CW01511359

Collage photos by Sue and Ros.

Look at Me

By Down's Syndrome North East

For everyone, past, present and future, who have
Down's syndrome, as well as their friends, families and carers.

Foreword

If this book had a second title it should be 'Inspiration'. Certainly, the stories that you read in these pages cannot fail to inspire us. They show the achievements of so many young people who are such an important part of our broad community.

Their self-inspiration has enabled them to tackle challenges that few of us will ever face, yet they present to us as positive and achieving members of our society.

Inspiration must also have been in the hearts and minds of parents, family, supporters, and carers who are an important part of the lives of these young people. Again facing hurdles and challenges that many must have thought insurmountable at one time.

And yet there must be further inspiration for all, in seeing how lives have changed and their continuing contribution as full members of our society. In a world that can seem very dark and savage to many, it is that inspiration from which we can learn and accept that so often there is a solution if we can but try.

Enjoy reading this book, you will be moved, and I hope inspired. Those who contributed to these pages certainly enjoyed their input, we can all learn many lessons in life from them.

Bill Midgley OBE, Patron of Down's Syndrome North East

Acknowledgements

This five-year journey of the Look at Me project would not have been possible without the enthusiastic and positive support of many people.

There is so much pride and joy in our book, Look at Me, our final part of the project.

Thanks to all our Look at Me models, now friends, and their families. The book would not exist without you.

Kayla Wren, our talented photographer, gave up hours and hours of time to take brilliant photos and bring our book to life. Despite all our demands on her time, she never complained and gave us complete permission to hassle her!

Our valued patron, Bill Midgley OBE, has been constant in his belief and support for our project. He provided us, as always, with sound advice and guidance to keep us on the right track.

Jenn Garside patiently worked with us throughout our changing decisions and requests and used her amazing graphic design skills to bring the book together in such an appealing way.

Lastly, we would like to give huge thanks to all our Down's Syndrome North East community. They have attended numerous planning meetings, given suggestions, and changed their plans at the last minute to help us.

We also want to thank the following people and organisations who have supported us so generously with donations to make our Look at Me book happen.

Bill Midgley OBE

In memory of Ada Midgley

Maving Taylor

Arnold Clark Community Fund

In memory of Joan Cope

The Barbour Foundation

The Rotary Club of Tyneside

The Rotary Club of Durham

In memory of Mick Pattison

Durham City Freemen

Benevolence Fund - Supported by local Freemasons

Like each snowflake, we are different
Like each grain of sand, unique
Like sunsets, we are awesome
Like each sunrise, magnifique
Like a flower, we have blossomed
Like a fine wine, we have aged
Like a long lost journal, we have passion on each page
Like all babies, we are beautiful
Like all rainbows, picturesque
Like all snowflakes, we are different
And exceptional at best

Tell me,
what do you see when you look at me?

Edited from a poem by Pamela Joyce Randolph

About 'Look at Me'

This book was created to raise awareness of Down's syndrome and promote inclusion.

Like everyone, children and adults with Down's syndrome are unique, valuable individuals who share the same wide range of emotions, experiences, and ambitions as all of us. Each page showcases the models' personalities, interests, and achievements and how they have grown and flourished over five years since the first photographs were taken in 2017.

The photographs encourage us to think about the unique and diverse qualities of people with Down's syndrome and to celebrate differences. Look at me! What do you see?

The Look at Me project

Look at Me began in 2017 when 37 volunteer models with Down's syndrome, living in the North East of England, were photographed by Kayla Wren. Her brother Nathan is one of the models. This formed a photo exhibition shown in many venues across the North East, including colleges and town halls during 2018 and 2019. It was seen by thousands of people and received a great deal of positive feedback.

This exhibition led to some members of Down's Syndrome North East (DSNE) creating and performing a dance called 'This is Me'. DSNE also held a conference to share how far the 'Look at Me' project had come, and members made a film, 'Look at Us', about our charity.

We hope there will be a copy of this book in every primary, first and special school in the North East. We also hope there will be copies in maternity units and our new baby gift boxes.

Comments from our Look at Me exhibition visitors

'A perfect dedication to individuality. A beautiful tribute.'

'Brightens up the day, and makes you smile!'

'Amazing - as a mum of a son with Down's syndrome, the pictures are totally inspiring - beautiful. xx'

'Beautiful photos. How wonderful to present what is often perceived as disability in such a positive and inclusive way.'

'Fabulous photos that really show individual personalities.'

'Your display is FAB. What beautiful people and truly inspiring' - dad of a beautiful young woman with Down's syndrome.'

'Amazing!!! Xx'

'Amazing, fantastic, love it! Well done!'

'So lovely to see that everyone is celebrated'

'Fabulous, the side of Down's syndrome we never get to see. The fun side!'

'Totally awesome. We're all part of one society, one world. Very inspiring.'

'Cool folk!'

'What a bunch of characters, FANTASTIC!'

'Personality, personality, personality. Wonderful photos!'

'Amazing photographs of amazing people. You should all be very proud of what you have achieved.'

'What do I see? Happiness, confidence, full of life, humour, strength, positivity, beauty, smiles, love, skills, ambition!'

'Fabulous photographs that really show individual personalities.'

'As a parent of a child with Down's syndrome my face lit up with delight as I saw all these beautiful people. Keep up the GREAT work!'

My favourite thing is water.
I love it. The sea, the pool, stepping stones over the river. I even love to play in the rain and jump in big, cold waves.

Do you know the song 'How far I'll go'? Moana is one of the best films ever.

I love sailing adventures on the high seas with my family. I'm learning to surf and I love to dive down really deep to look for treasure.

Is it a mermaid? Is it a seal? No, it's Frances.

Hi I'm Stephanie and I like to sing for fun.

I also enjoy theatre, both performing and watching.

I like keeping fit with gym and Zumba too.

Rachel likes going fast, having snowball fights and hot chocolate.

Luke's favourite thing in the world was Peppa Pig.

Now, it is being at school and reading books. He is a little thrill seeker and loves going high and fast.

I can hula hoop for over 1 minute!

Harriet learnt to hula hoop by watching other kids at school then doing lots of practise.

She loves to show off her skills and takes great pleasure that no-one in the family is anywhere near as good at it as she is.

Hi I'm Katherine.

I've got a season ticket for Newcastle Falcons rugby team. You can hear me cheering from the stand.

I love wearing my Falcons top, waving my flag and watching the after match entertainment.

I always wanted to work at Marks and Spencer's in their coffee shop as I used to go there with my mum.

After work experience I was given a temporary contract and then my job was made permanent.

I love seeing my regular customers and having a chat with them.

I clean the tables, fill the dishwasher, take the food to the customers and I make a very good latte.

I love talking to my work colleagues.

I feel very proud to wear my Marks and Spencer's uniform.

Keep practising to be a knockout!

Hi, I'm Megan.

Doing forward rolls every day is fun.

Ishaan loves dancing.

He is a Sunderland fan.

He enjoys talking to anyone and everyone.

Cakes and Burger King make him very happy.

His favourite line that we hear often is 'I love my life!'.

Hi, Andrew here.

I'm 43 and I'm fit and healthy.

I love dancing and I like to party.

I also love 007 James Bond and I enjoy being an uncle.

My dream job!

My name is Craig.

I'm good at working with tools.

From one legend to another.

Hello, my name is William and I love going to school. I have lots of friends.

I enjoy listening to music, watching Disney movies, and going out with my friends, especially to the theatre and parties.

We are Lynsey and Paul.
We were excited and happy to get
married in 2014. Now we live in our
very own house with a garden.

Hello, I'm Brent.
I've got lots of friends at DSNE. I'm a good dancer. I'm a good person. I like helping other people. I like to chill and relax in my room.

Hi, I am Lily.
I love dancing to the Wiggles and listening to party music.
I really enjoy going to the playground and my favourite toys are Mickey Mouse and Minnie Mouse.

Hi, I'm Callum and I'm 18.
I love music and to sing and drum along
to my favourite bands, mainly Green Day,
Coldplay and Queen.
I spend most of my spare time on my
electric drum kit.

Hi, I'm Charlotte and I'm 6 years old.

I love gymnastics and swimming.

My family and pet cats are really important to me.

My favourite thing is going on days out or holidays with my family.

I love playing with Marvel figures in my spare time and reading books.

I have a swing in my garden and always ask to be pushed 'high in the sky'.

Harry loves playing with toy cars.
He loves the hosepipe in the garden
and chasing his brother to wet him.
'No' is his favourite word.
Harry loves climbing and cuddles.

I love Peppa Pig.

My name is Ella. I love Brownies; we play games, make things and sing songs. I love being with my Brownie friends.

I'm Charlie.

I love playing the Switch. It's so fun.
My favourite game is Mario Kart because I love it.
I like going at top speed.

I'm Sophie, I amaze my family every day.

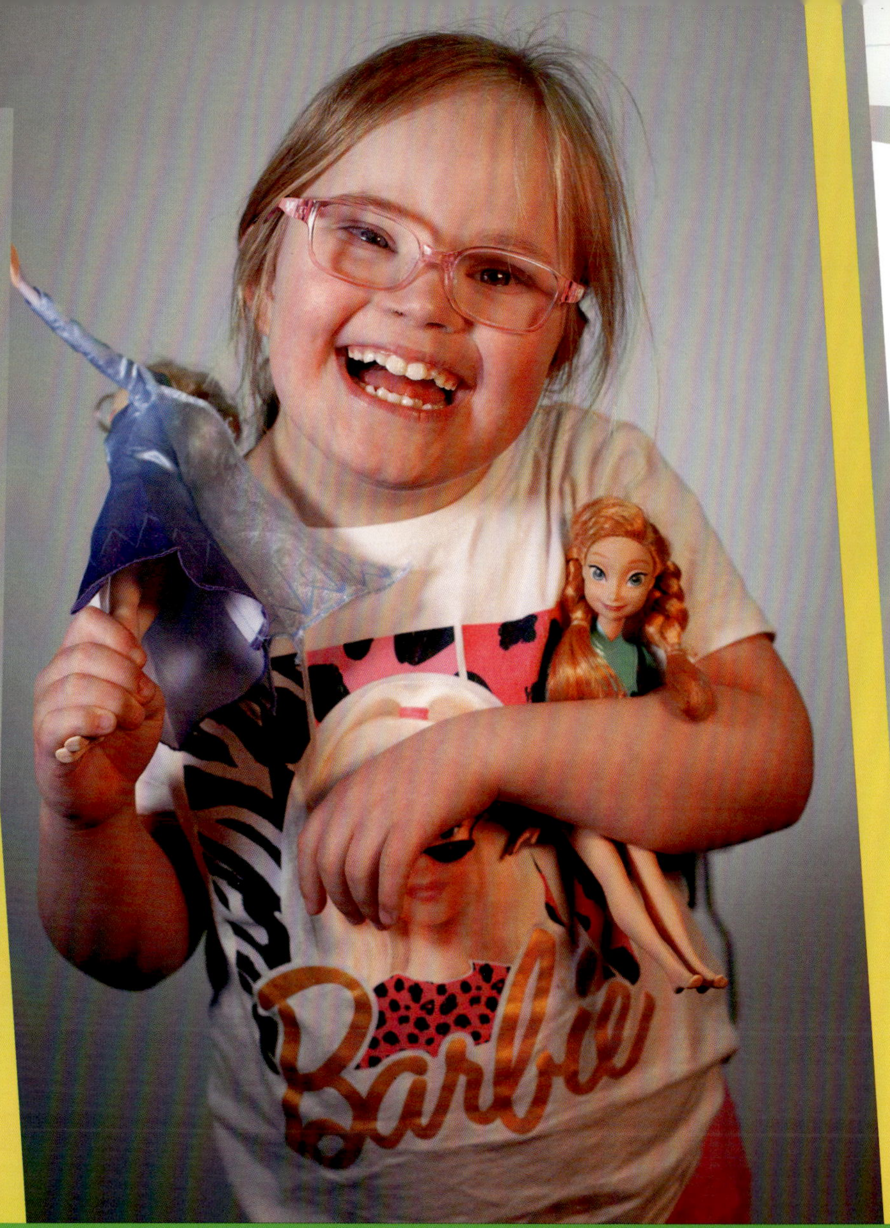

I'm doing well at school.
My love of plastic toys has moved on to Barbie – big style.
I keep Barbie's dream house tidier than my own bedroom.
I love my sister, cousins and all my friends, oh, AND SWIMMING.

Hi, Emma here.

This is me looking happy and glamorous in my long dress.

My hobbies are singing, dancing and drama. I love performing on stage with my drama group. I also like going out for a nice meal or to the pub with my friends.

'Aye aye, Captain Gareth here.'

I go sailing every week. My steering at the tiller is awesome and I aim for the buoys. I won the Club cup for enthusiasm and got my Bronze award. I'm working towards the Silver. I have to learn some tricky knots and name parts of the boat.

My name is Prentice.

I feel good when I'm dressed up smartly.

I like James Bond, Dick and Dom, Tin Arts and school.

I loved my holiday in Disney and I love my girlfriend.

I'm Lucy.
I like music and maths at school and I have lots of friends there.
I enjoy doing handstands in the swimming pool, gymnastics and I love my theatre group, True Colours, because I love being on stage.

School is very important to Amelia.
She dislikes school holidays.

Amelia loves exploring the garden in
all weathers and playing on her trampoline.
Like lots of her friends, she loves Peppa Pig.

Archie's favourite teams are Barcelona and England.
He feels really good when they score goals.
He likes to play football in the garden or on big, open fields.
When he scores, he copies Ronaldo's celebration.

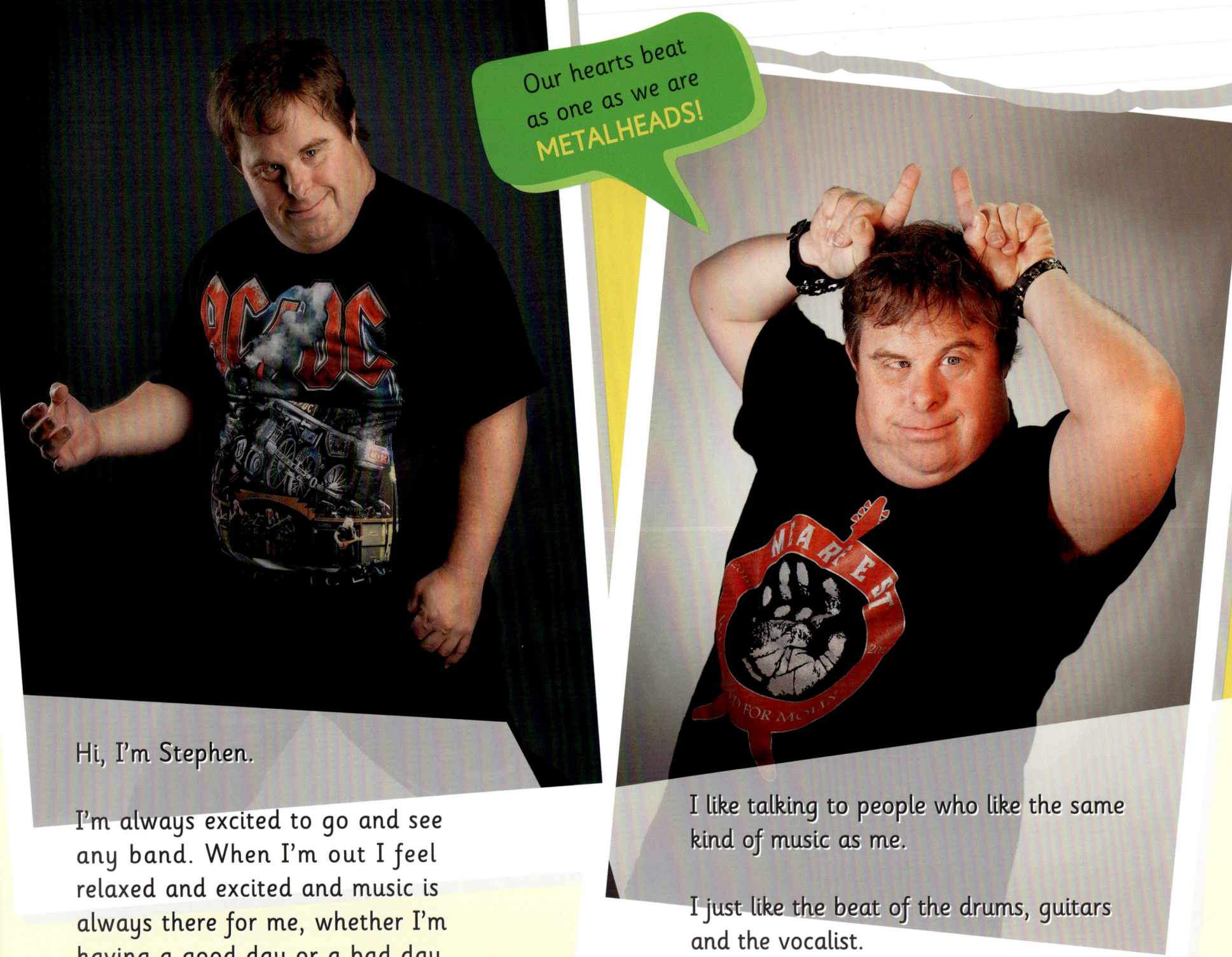

Our hearts beat as one as we are METALHEADS!

Hi, I'm Stephen.

I'm always excited to go and see any band. When I'm out I feel relaxed and excited and music is always there for me, whether I'm having a good day or a bad day.

I like talking to people who like the same kind of music as me.

I just like the beat of the drums, guitars and the vocalist.

Hi, I'm Lillie.

My mum works in ASDA and makes the best cheese and pepperoni pizzas.
I'm wearing an apron and hat like my mum and sprinkled the cheese on top of the pizza.

I love colouring in, Coca-Cola and sharks.

My name is Nathan.

I love wrestling and have always done so since
I was small. I would love to be a wrestler.

Ribbons are Leo's favourite toy. He loves the feel of the material, the bright colours and the shadows they make.

Leo loves to play in water, splashing in the bath or hot tub, or learning to swim. The swimming pool is his favourite place to be.

Kiai!

A week after this photo was taken
Liv had her grading.

'At grading I got an orange stripe,
I felt super excited.
Karate makes me feel good.'

Joshua is all about superheroes.
He will say, 'Web web,' pose like Spider-Man and shoot webs.
He often says, 'Hulk smash' when he is scared or angry.
Joshua grabs his Captain America shield shouting, 'America!'
as he fights and gets you to hit his shield.

My name is Finn.

I love teasing and playing with my sister, Lucy, and my dog, Floyd.

I absolutely love superheroes; Superman and Spider-Man are the best.

Toy Story has always been my favourite movie. I have often thought my Buzz Lightyears could fly and threw them out of the window.

My favourite food is pizza and ice cream. I enjoy school but my favourite place to be is at home with my family in my pjs.

I'm Alexandra and I love to dance.
I like to choreograph my own moves
and dances.

I do modern and contemporary dance.

It makes me feel happy and I love to perform
on stage and be in the 'light'.
I have been teaching some students dance
exercises in workshops.
It has been a good opportunity for me and
I have really loved it and want to do more.

Hello, I'm Matthew.
I work with my team buddies, we make parts for aeroplanes.

I am holding my special paperwork stamp on my photo.
I love getting paid and I use my money to go out for meals with my family and friends.
I am a professional dancer with The National Youth Dance Company.
P.S. I want to be a professional pianist; this is my next dream.

About DSNE

Down's Syndrome North East is a registered charity that supports children and adults of all ages with Down's syndrome living in the North East of England. We provide social activities, workshops, and outings for children, adults, and their families. We also offer advice, support, and training for parents and carers and promote awareness of Down's syndrome throughout the region.

DSNE covers Northumberland, Tyneside, Wearside, County Durham, and Teesside, and is entirely run by volunteers.

About Down's Syndrome

Down's syndrome is a condition that people are born with. It's also known as Trisomy 21 because there is an extra copy of the 21st chromosome in each cell in the body. It's part of the person, for all of their life. People with Down's syndrome are individuals with unique strengths and challenges, with their own personalities and characteristics. It might take people with Down's syndrome longer to learn new things. They might need a bit more help but, like everyone, people with Down's syndrome are lifelong learners.

Did you know?

- We prefer 'person first' language. A person has Down's syndrome. Not 'a Down's baby' or 'he is Down's'. Instead please say: 'This is Alice. She has Down's syndrome.'

- Down's syndrome is the most common, naturally occurring, chromosomal condition. Around 1 in every 800 babies born in the UK has Down's syndrome.

- People have Down's syndrome. They don't suffer from Down's syndrome. Many adults and children who have Down's syndrome will tell you that they love their lives.

- Down's syndrome is a condition, not a disease or illness. It does not need to be cured or treated.

- Many adults with Down's syndrome can live in their own homes, have relationships, have jobs, and certainly have great lives, as you can see in this book.

- People who have Down's syndrome are not always happy, and have the same range of emotion as everyone has.

- Some people with Down's syndrome can have quite complex needs and may need more help to learn and do things.

- People who have Down's syndrome are just as individual and different from one another as every one is. When you have met one person with Down's syndrome, you have met one person with Down's syndrome! People with Down's syndrome do share some common physical characteristics, but are most definitely not all the same.

- World Down's syndrome day is celebrated every year on March 21st. The aim is to raise awareness about Down's syndrome, as well as celebrate the lives of everyone who has Down's syndrome.

Collage photos by Sue and Ros.